*"**Doggy's Busy Day** is dedicated to my family who helped encourage Ella the Doggy to "ham it up" for the pictures included in this book."*

Jayne Flaagan

Husky Publishing

East Grand Forks, MN 56721

email:djflaagan@gra.mido.net

Praise for *"Doggy's Busy Day"*

"A sweet book for children that takes them on an adventure with Ella the dog. Because of the format and the questions asked, it as interactive as one can have in a book. Children can go on an adventure with Ella as they can see themselves right in the story. Whether the young reader has a dog or not, this is a delightful book that will bring joy to many young hearts."

~ Christiana Caeliss

"*Doggy's Busy Day*" by Jayne Flaagan is an appealing book for young children, supported by photos of her adorable husky dog. Don't let the simple format fool you into thinking this is a passive read. The questions embedded in each page invite engagement and consideration by the youngsters and their adult reading companions relevant to their own life, possibly extending into more complex conversations over time. What's more, the book is structured to take the doggie through a normal day, which can provide a parallel support structure for the reader. These elements are crucial in early learning success. Enjoy!

~ Donna Kim-Brand

"Jayne Flaagan's book "*Doggy's Busy Day*" is a charming visual treat, featuring the photogenic husky, Ella. Filled with full-page color photos of Ella in numerous lovable poses, the book asks young readers to notice the similarities between the pup and themselves. This book is sure to be requested over and over by any child."

~ Hiyaguha Cohen

Because we appreciate you as a reader, please accept our free, no-obligation gifts to you, which include...

1. **FREE** audio book of *"Doggy's Busy Day"* *to download*

2. **FREE** coloring pages of Ella to print and color

    You will be able to access both the audio book and the coloring pages immediately!

To receive your free gifts and learn more about *"Ella the Doggy"* books, click below!

www.ellathedoggy.com

This is Ella the Doggy.

She has two eyes.
She has two ears.
She has one nose.
She has one mouth.

Just like you.

Ella has four legs and one tail.

How many legs do you have?

Do you have a tail?

When Ella wakes up
in the morning,
she gives herself a
very big stretch!

How does that feel when you stretch?

Ella is very hungry when she wakes up, so she gets ready for breakfast.

She is licking her lips because she is so hungry!

Do you wear a bib when you eat?

Sometimes Ella will sit up and ask for food.

She cannot say "*please*" because
doggies cannot talk.

What do you say when you want something?

Ella eats her breakfast from a white bowl.

The bowl is all chewed up because Ella has sharp teeth and she likes to play with it.

Doggies drink lots of water too.
Ella drinks from a blue bowl.

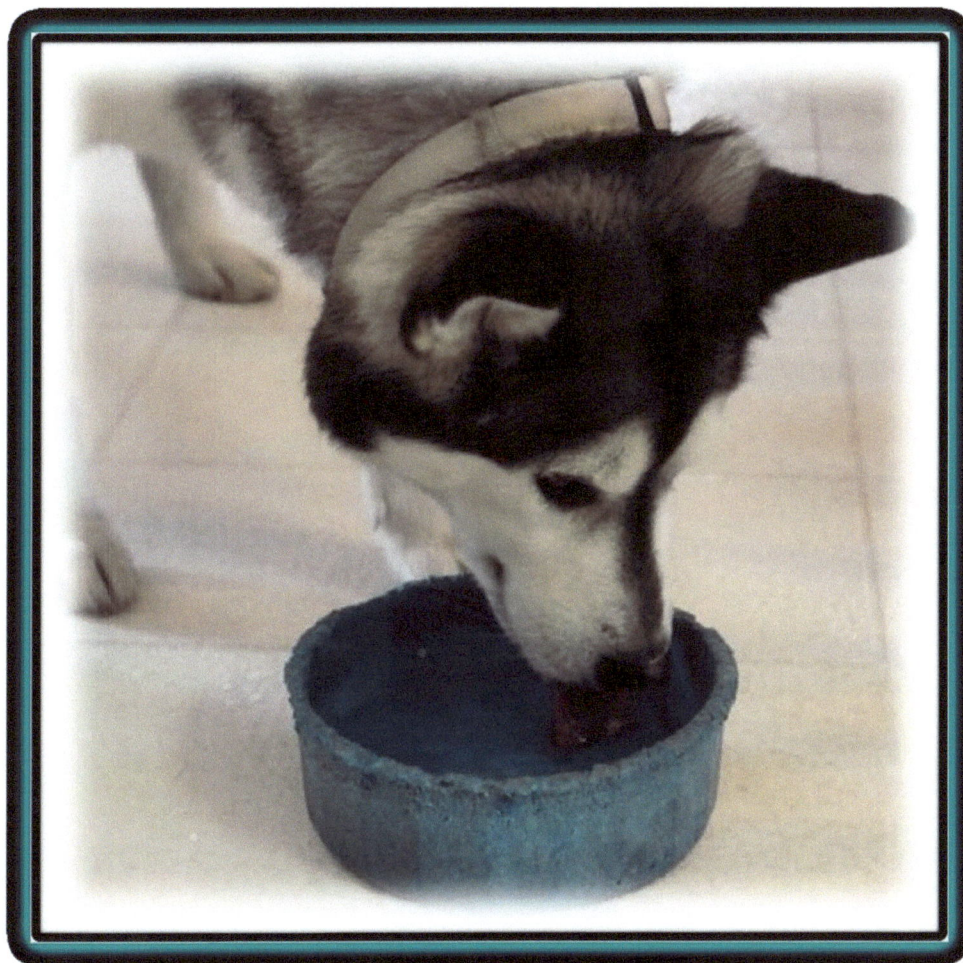

What do you use to drink water?

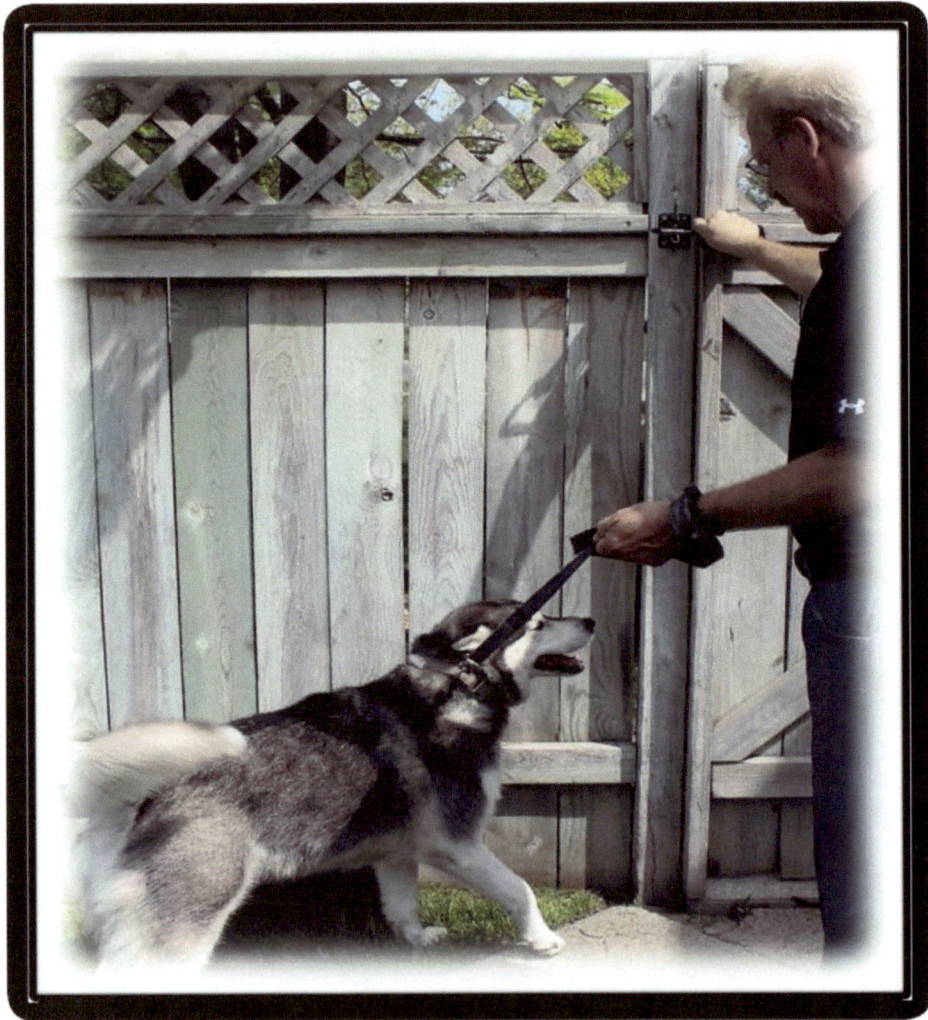

Ella is going on a walk now.
She is very excited!

Ella loves to walk outside in the fresh air.

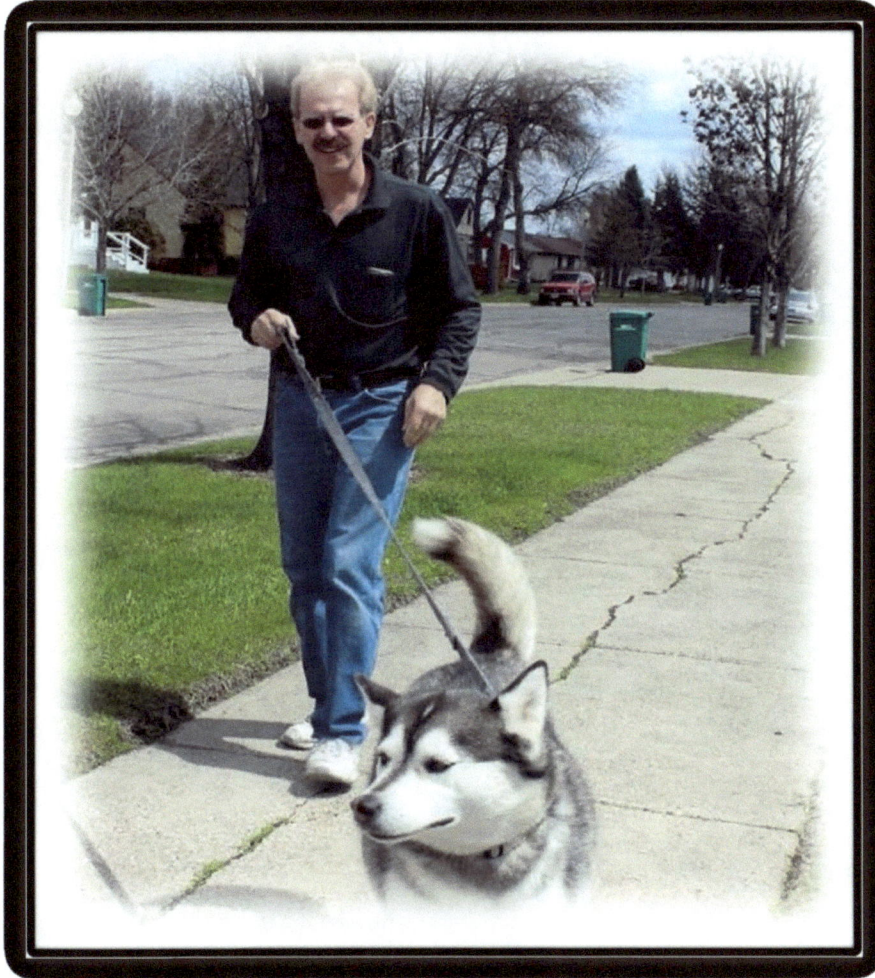

What do you do to exercise so
you can grow big and strong?

Even when it is cold
outside, Ella takes a walk.

Do you have snow where you live?

After her walk Ella is tired,
so she naps in the sun.

Where do you rest?

Ella feels lonely right now.

She wants someone to play with.

Now Ella is happy because she sees a friend!

What does your face look like when you are sad?

How does your face look when you are happy?

This is Ella when she was smaller.
She is playing with her friend Daisy.

What are the names of your friends?

Sometimes Ella has picnics with her people friends.

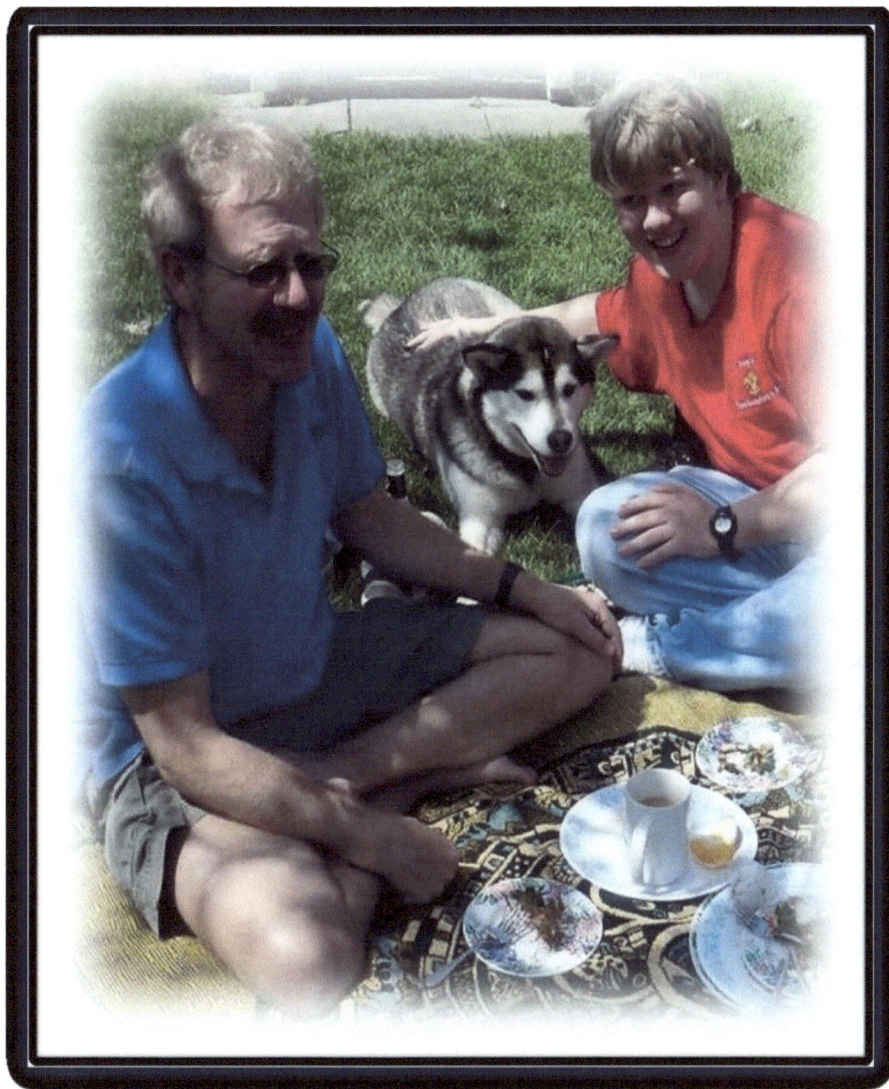

What do you eat when you go on a picnic?

Look who is being silly!

What do you do when you act silly?

Ella likes to play games.

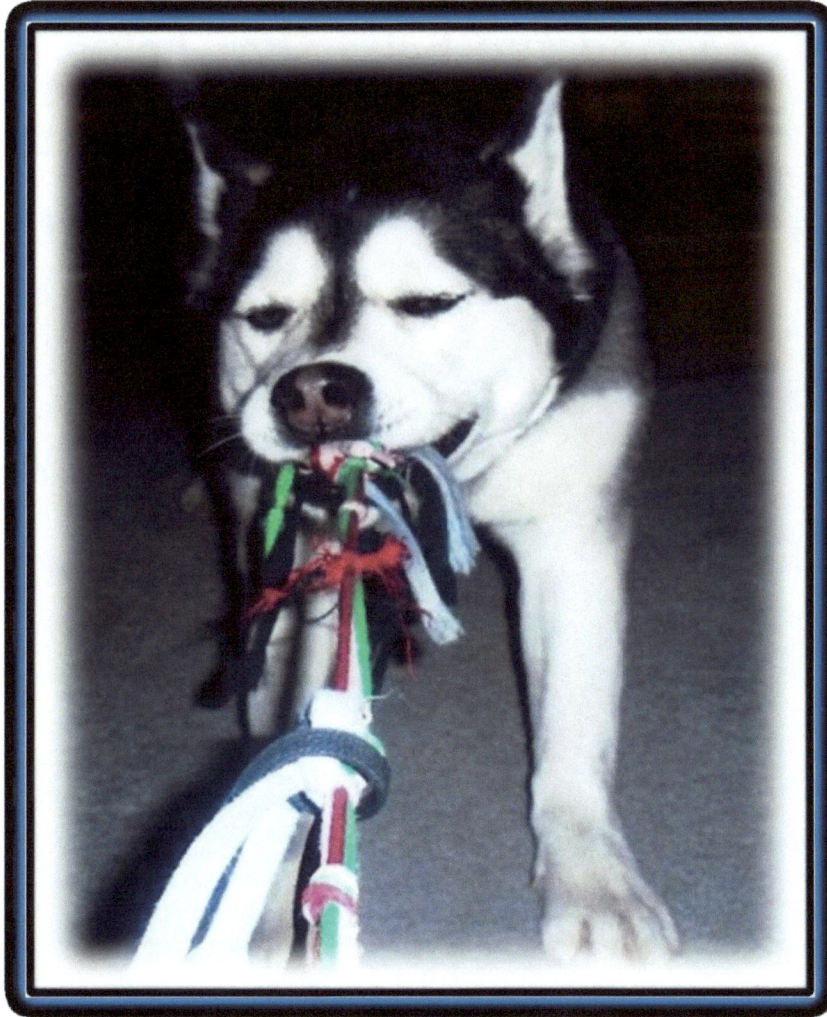

One of her favorite games is called "*Tug-of War.*"

Here is Ella playing another game.

She has to find the hand that holds her treat.

Can you help her find the treat?

Ella is a good dancer.

How do you dance?

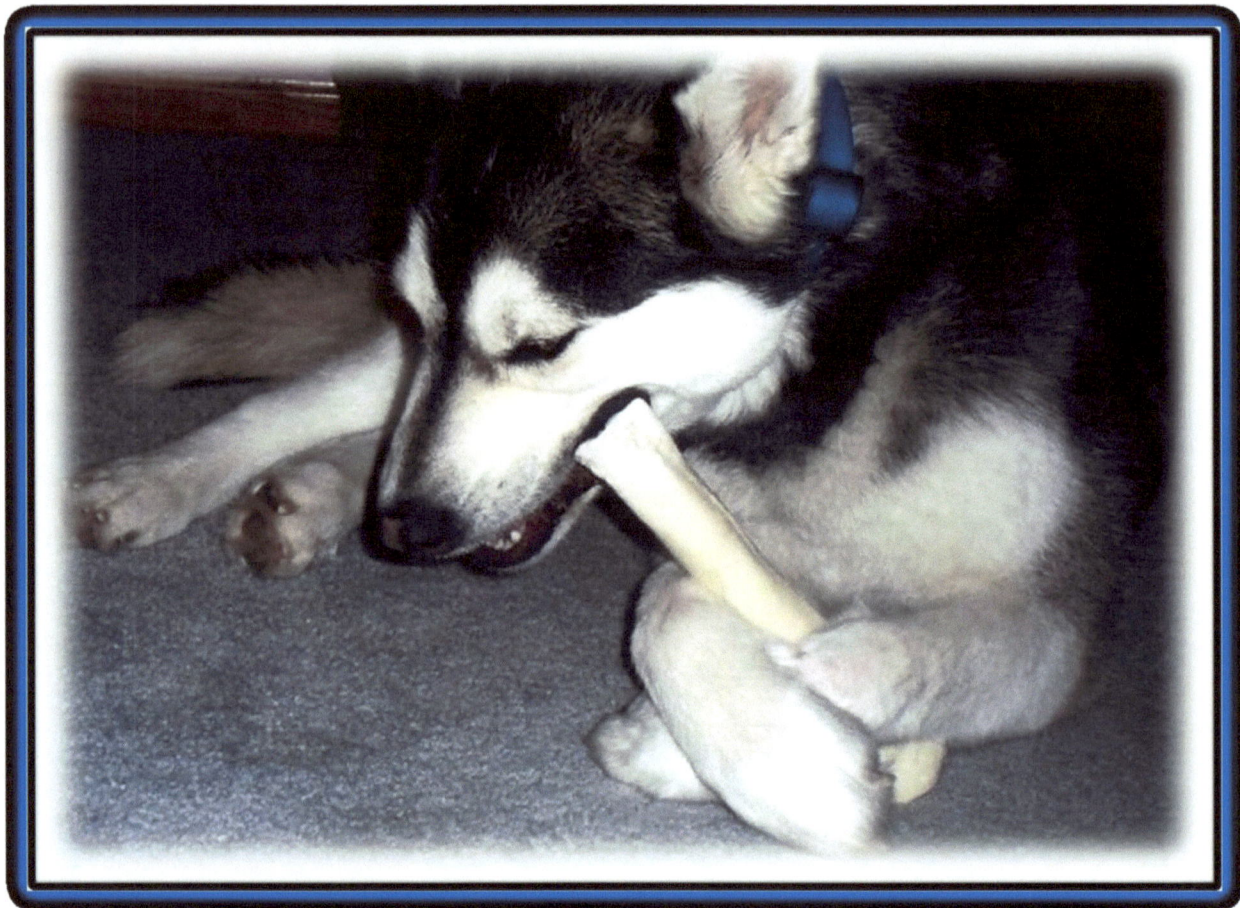

Sometimes Ella just likes to
rest and chew on her bone...

and sometimes she plays with a ball.

Ella likes to give
kisses to people...

with her long tongue!

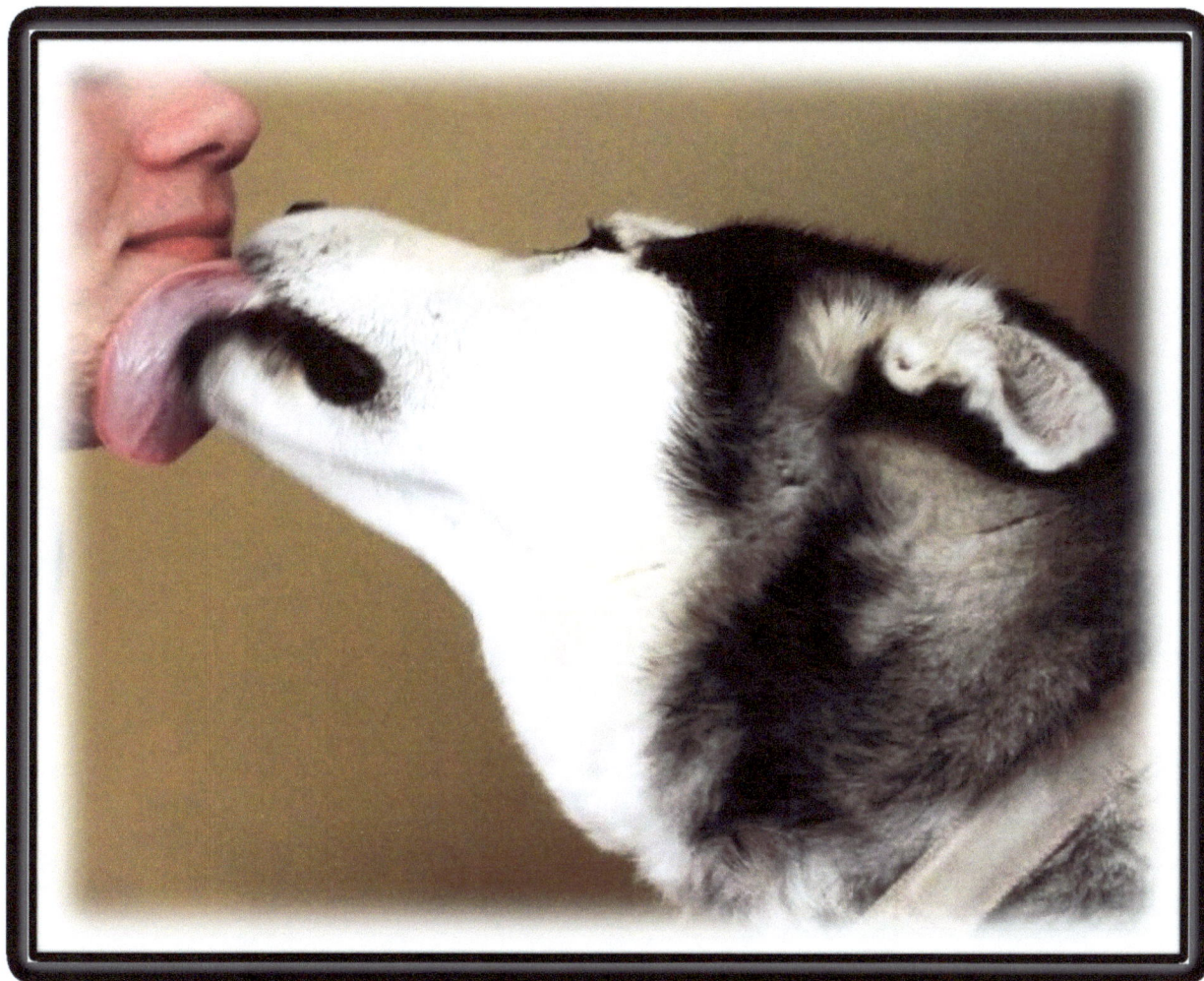

Ella likes to hug people too.

Today Ella is going
for a ride in the car.

Oh no! She is not wearing a seat belt!

When she meets new people,
Ella shakes with her paw...

and she gives a "*high five*" when she is excited!

Do you shake with a paw or with a hand?
Do you know how to give "*high fives?*"

It has been a very busy day for Ella.

But wait...

...where is she going?

Here is Ella!

She is looking out the window.

Ella is thinking about all of the things that will keep her busy tomorrow!

About the Author

Jayne Flaagan grew up in North Dakota and made the big move to Minnesota many years ago. She lives with her husband and her goofy dog named Ella. She also has three adult children.

Flaagan has degrees in Advertising/Public Relations, Elementary Education and French. Her experience includes a background of over 30 years in Elementary and Early Childhood education, as well an extensive expertise in writing for many different publications and in several different genres. She thoroughly enjoys writing for young readers.

The author can speak Spanish, loves to travel, read, do crossword puzzles, and spend time with her family, as well as having various other hobbies and past times. She is an extremely avid fan of the sunshine, which makes Minnesota winters a bit too long for her liking.

Books have always been a huge part of her life and reading to children is something that she feels is critical to every child's learning experience. Between her jobs and raising her children, she estimates that she has probably read over a million books to children over the years!

Jayne Flaagan grew up on a farm with a Husky for a pet and she has many fond memories of him. When it was time to get a dog for her own family, she knew that it had to be a Husky. Huskies are fun, lovable and have lots of energy. Ella has provided so much joy and entertainment for her own family that Flaagan decided she wanted to share Ella with other families. Thus, "*Ella the Doggy*" book series was born!

"Ella the Doggy" books
(available in both Kindle and paperback)

Doggy's Busy Day

Doggy Finds Her Bone

Doggy Loves Autumn

Doggy's Minnesota Winter

Doggy Celebrates Christmas

Doggy's Favorite Colors

Where is Doggy?

Doggy Gets a Bath

El Día Ocupado de la Perrita/Doggy's Buy Day
(Bilingual book in both Spanish and English)

Hundis Aufregender Tag/Doggy's Busy Day
(Bilingual book in both German and English)

La Journée Chargée de la Petite/Doggy's Busy Day
(Bilingual book in both French and English)

Dogii bijii dei wanko no era/Doggy's Busy Day
(Bilingual book in both Japanese and English)

Pracowity Dzień Pieska/Doggy's Busy Day
(Bilingual book in both Polish and English)

Ella the Doggy

www.ingramcontent.com/pod-product-compliance
Lightning Source LLC
Chambersburg PA
CBHW041237040426
42445CB00004B/55